ESSENTIALS OF NURSING MANAGEMENT

Financial Management

Geoffrey Woodhall
and
Alan Stuttard

MACMILLAN

First published 1999 by
MACMILLAN PRESS LTD
Houndmills, Basingstoke, Hampshire RG21 6XS
and London
Companies and representatives
throughout the world

ISBN 0–333–59369–3 paperback

A catalogue record for this book is available from the British Library.

This book is printed on paper suitable for recycling and made from fully managed and sustained forest sources.

10 9 8 7 6 5 4 3 2 1
08 07 06 05 04 03 02 01 00 99

Editing and origination by
Aardvark Editorial, Mendham, Suffolk

Printed and bound in Great Britain by
Creative Print and Design (Wales), Ebbw Vale

Dedicated to

*Joan Corcoran, Manager, Occupational Therapy Services,
Royal Preston Hospital*

*Eileen Jones, Business Manager, Directorate of Obstetrics
and Gynaecology,
Queen's Medical Centre, Nottingham*

and

*Ada Thompson, Head of Community Nursing, Lancaster
whose enthusiasm and professionalism inspired this book*

Contents

Contents

Contents

List of Figures and Tables

Figures

Tables

Acknowledgements

This book is the result of a long period of reflection about finance in the health service. The authors would like to thank everyone involved in that period of reflection, especially Richenda Milton-Thompson and staff at Macmillan.

Thanks are also due to Professor Graham Kelly and Dr Roger Kendle for allowing us access to multi-disciplinary teams over a long period of years, and to Professor John Blake and Diane Roberts for their cheerful and unobtrusive encouragement. Finally, the greatest thanks to Angela Elsworth, Maria Wang, Penny Heaney and Sadiya Ali, without whose help this book would have remained a dream.

We hope that you, the reader, will write to us with improvements and suggestions for future editions, and we wish you every good wish in your professional career.

Introduction

Providing a service in the health service is the paramount purpose of most people's careers. Everyone fits together into a team which can deliver a programme of health care, either prevention, cure or alleviation of suffering. Throughout your career, you are building up skills which matter, so that when a task has to be done, or an emergency has to be faced, those skills are brought into play. In such circumstances, money is not an issue; the pattern of care and treatment is what really matters. The focus of a hospital is on getting the best pattern of care or the best pattern of response to what the patient needs. Where does money come into the provision of that care?

In a sense, money is the blood which flows through the organisation of care. It is vital for supporting a hospital, but it is controlled by a limited number of people and it is regarded as a technical operation. Fortunately, many nurses and doctors manage to exist on a daily basis concentrating on care patterns for their patients. Money tends to be regarded as an unnecessary complication, a source of annoyance even , or a dirty word not to be mentioned in polite circles!

The hospital functions primarily according to the values of its senior staff and managers. They will at some time consider the totality of care which can be bought and provided. They also allocate the money available so that the right proportions of work can be done to meet the needs of the community which the hospital serves.

Accounting in this sort of scenario is done behind closed doors, and is of more interest to the technical people who do it, rather than being of everyday application to people involved in delivering a service within an operating theatre, a ward, a clinic or an out-patients or community nursing situation.

So, the big questions are:

Why finance? Where does it fit in? When do you need to know something about it?

This book seeks to give an overview of how finance fits into the health service. In your future career you may, at some point, be faced with a meeting or a discussion or a negotiating position where someone in the room speaks authoritatively about money and the jargon is strange. Some sort of prior knowledge of the subject is needed to keep abreast of the discussion. It may be in a new job situation, setting up a unit for the first time, trying to find the level of funds needed to run it, or it may be in negotiating a different pattern of care on a ward that you need an understanding of how budgets are devised in order to equip the ward with the best chance of running satisfactorily without constraints on activity or on the levels and standard of patient care. This book takes you through the overview of how money is held and controlled within the system, just like blood running through the body, and how it is pumped and monitored so that all parts of the organisation receive sufficient to keep alive.

A glossary at the end of the book helps explain the terminology. Good luck on your tour round the money maze!

Chapter 1 An Introduction to Finance in the Health Service: The Role of Central Government

Structure of the NHS

In the UK, the government of the day has the power to change its policy by introducing new legislation in Parliament. In 1989 the government heralded the largest single set of reforms in the National Health Service (NHS) since 1948 by the publication of two White Papers in 1989: *Working for Patients* (DoH) and *Caring for People* (Secretaries of State for Health, Social Security) and a new structure was introduced, operating from 1 April 1991. The structure is headed by the Secretary of State for Health, who is answerable to Parliament, and has a place in the Cabinet.

The *Department of Health* has the role of being a department of professionals, headed by the Secretary of State, which has the responsibility of controlling the management of the health service through long-term and short-term plans, and by a continual overview of the service.

The *NHS Policy Board* is chaired by the Secretary of State and is a means of developing strategy for the NHS, and of setting the objectives of the NHS Executive.

The *NHS Executive* comprises health service professionals with specific responsibilities for implementation of policies, and answerable to the Policy Board.

District Health Authorities (DHAs) were in existence prior to the NHS reforms. Following the reforms, DHAs now have a role as purchasers of health services.

NHS Trusts are a result of the reforms; they represent hospitals which have decided to become self-governing.

The structure is shown in Figure 1.1.

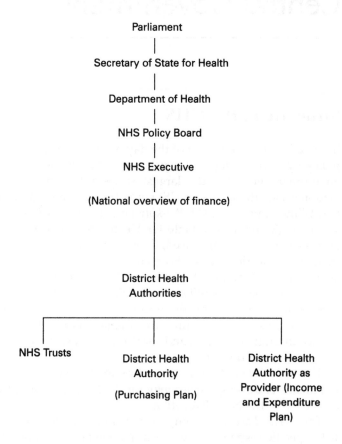

Parliament

|

Secretary of State for Health

|

Department of Health

|

NHS Policy Board

|

NHS Executive

|

(National overview of finance)

District Health
Authorities

NHS Trusts

District Health
Authority

(Purchasing Plan)

District Health
Authority as
Provider (Income
and Expenditure
Plan)

Figure 1.1   Structure of the NHS and flow of funds

Financial Planning at a National Level

The money required to run the NHS represents the largest single category of expenditure in the budget of central government. As such it has to be closely planned and controlled, and approved by Parliament. Before receiving Parliamentary approval, the First Secretary of the Treasury has to negotiate with ministers about the claims of their departments for future spending. The Cabinet has to consider the rate of growth of different departments, and the Chancellor of the Exchequer has to assess the state of the economy and its ability to produce sufficient revenue from taxation to support all the government's spending proposals. The summary of these proposals is published as the 'Autumn Statement'; this is an important indicator of the assumptions which have been built into the plans: for example, it draws attention to areas where 'new money' may be available for developing new services.

Planned expenditure is divided into two categories:

- *Current* refers to on-going regular day-to-day spending on pay, salaries, supplies and expenses of the NHS.
- *Capital* refers to a large schemes of construction, land purchase, or buying vehicles and equipment, where the benefit from that spending will extend for a period beyond the year in which the spending actually occurred.

An extract of the government's expenditure plans as reported to Parliament in March 1997 is shown in Table 1.1.

Table 1.1 Department of Health, central government's own expenditure

	1997/98	
	Current expenditure £millions	*Capital expenditure £millions*
Health, community health and related services	24,368	1,315
Family health services	7,873	–
Departmental administration	277	8
Central Health and miscellaneous services	519	8
Total voted by Parliament:	33,037	1,331

Source: Departmental Report (Cm 3612)

This extract from the government's own expenditure plans illust-
rates an important requirement of the health service, the need to
summarise information to convey the totality of expenditure, the
requirements made on the public purse, for health provision in
the community. Throughout this book, you will find summaries
of information, and the task of an accountant within the health
service is to analyse, collate, and summarise financial information. Hospitals prepare data which are given to business
managers, who may delegate some of the responsibility to groups
of physicians or nurses within a directorate. Data are provided as
an estimate, are analysed at the point where money is spent, and
monitored subsequently to find out where variations have
occurred between what is planned and what was spent. Data
collection is useful at different levels of decision making: at the
point of service delivery, at ward or clinic level, at directorate
level, at hospital level, and at national level. People working
within the health service need to have a common understanding
at all levels so that they can communicate effectively.

Central government is aware that the provision of health
services is a politically sensitive topic, because the government,
through its plans and strategies, is affecting the lives of many
people. As individuals, people want the right pattern of treatment and the right pattern of care when they become ill. The
Cabinet has to balance the needs of health against the needs of
other departments, for example education, defence, prisons and
so on. The Treasury acts as the data collecting agency through
which all this financial information passes. A Treasury minister,
the Chief Secretary to the Treasury, has to reconcile the government's political aspirations with the availability of funds
through taxation, and has to communicate with departmental
ministers, who are the politically appointed chiefs of spending
departments, the extent to which their spending needs and
priorities will be met.

Some aspirations are met immediately, others are regarded as
priority and, over the life of a Parliament, both the Treasury
ministers and the departmental ministers are accountable
through Parliament for their strategies and decisions on service
delivery and maintenance of standards within agreed spending
patterns, authorised by Parliament. At the end of the Parliamentary term of office, usually every five years, the electorate has

the opportunity of indicating its agreement or otherwise of the government's record and performance through a simple cross on a ballot paper.

In a democracy, the driving force which leads a person to vote may be a combination of reactions or feelings that the voter wants 'more of the same', or a positive change to 'something different', with the anticipation that a change is 'a change for the better'. In the period prior to an election, parties, both of government and opposition, will seek to put forward their plans as a manifesto, and each of these documents will be analysed publically through the press, television, and other media sources. Ultimately, voters will decide whether or not to use their vote, and which way to exercise it.

While in office, the party of government can communicate its plans through consultation papers (known as *Green Papers*), or can make definite proposals for change, (known as *White Papers*), and can issue press releases through the media, explaining present or proposed policies.

An opposition party can support, modify, or oppose these proposals when they come to Parliamentary consideration, through the means of select committees, or through the committee stage in Parliament. The House of Commons in committee can give detailed consideration, line by line if necessary, to proposed legislation embodying government policy.

When Parliament is dissolved, and an election is pending, those processes cease, and the public at large is able to judge the merits of existing policies and the proposals put forward for the future in the parties' manifestos. We do not know what influences people to vote, but health, as the biggest single spending service, must feature somewhere in the public's perception of the government's overall performance. For this reason, health is a politically sensitive and important topic to the government of the day. The descriptions in the following pages of how the health service is organised reflect the current position at the time of writing. It is possible that changes may be made in the future to the structure and processes described.

Financial Planning at a Local Level

In order for the NHS Executive to have an overview of finance, it is necessary for each DHA and NHS Trust to provide financial information. Following the reforms of 1991, which were incorporated in the NHS and Community Care Act 1990, the responsibility for health care was divided between 'purchasers' and 'providers'.

Purchasers

DHAs become responsible for assessing the needs of their resident populations, and securing health services for them. So the role of the DHA was to review the health needs of their geographical areas, by research, by examining patterns of illness, patterns of care provided in the past, current caseloads and waiting lists, and through annual contracts securing sufficient care for such a load to be handled within a twelve-month period, ending on 31 March.

Providers

An NHS Trust hospital would be the main provider of health care. Trust hospitals would deliver services to 'purchasers' in accordance with a pre-arranged contract. The contract would state the volume of patients to be treated, and would specify the quality of care and the quantity or amount of care to be provided.

Managed Competition

The separation of responsibilities between 'purchasers' and 'providers' introduced the practice of managed competition into the NHS. The government, through the 1990 Act, redefined the role of DHAs, and placed them within the environment of managed competition. The White Paper *Working for Patients* expressed the arrangements as follows:

In future, each District Health Authority's duty will be to buy the best service it can from its own hospitals, from other authorities' hospitals, from self-governing hospitals, or from the private health sector.

Hospitals for their part will have to satisfy districts that they [that is the hospitals] are providing the best and most efficient service. They [that is hospitals] will be free to offer their services to other district health authorities. (extract from paragraph 4.23)

The introduction of 'managed competition' meant that the provision of health services was not going to be a 'free for all', in which the unrestrained market forces would permanently destabilise the provision of care, which had taken many years to develop, but instead, competition was to be introduced steadily and gradually.

The existence of contracts would strengthen the information available to DHAs as purchasers and would create a stronger planning environment in which information on activity within the NHS would be passed to the DoH via the NHS Executive.

NHS Trusts

A Trust is a self-governing unit within the NHS, but independent of a DHA. A Trust earns its income from contracts, and retains any financial surplus as a result of its income being greater than its expenditure in any financial year. The reverse also applies: a Trust may incur a deficit if its expenditure is greater than its income in any financial year. A Trust is not confined to a hospital: other aspects of the NHS can apply for Trust status, for example:

- ambulance services
- services for a particular group, such as patients with mental illness, or mental handicap
- a single, major acute hospital
- an acute hospital located in a district with associated community services
- all community and priority care services provided in a district.

Each Trust has a line or a duty of direct accountability through the NHS Executive to the Secretary of State for Health. They are independent of regional or district management. They have perpetual succession; they are an independent legal entity, with power to determine policies, and to monitor the execution of those policies in line with agreed guidelines.

Business Plans for NHS Trusts

As a Trust is independently governed, but is within the NHS. It has to report to the NHS Executive and prepare an annual business plan covering three years. The plans must show:

- the assumptions about the purchasing power of the authorities with whom the Trust has contractual arrangements
- plans for future capital developments and how these will be funded
- assumptions about changes in external conditions, for example patient numbers, inflation, interest rates.

The NHS Executive will be able to assess over a period of years how closely a Trust is performing in comparison to its plans, and will be able to form an opinion on the accuracy or reliability of plans from each Trust.

Income estimates are based on the volume of expected work multiplied by the price of each item of service.

Expenditure estimates are based on accurate costing of each function or clinical specialism. The process of building up a budget is explained in Chapter 6.

Types of Contract

In order to establish a contractual relationship between 'purchaser' and 'provider', three main types of contract are available and in regular use in the NHS.

Block Contract

This indicates the types of services to be provided, and an annual contract price, payable in instalments, entitling the purchaser to refer patients resident within the area of the DHA to the provider for treatment.

Cost and Volume Contract

This is similar to a block contract but has an indication of volume, permitting the purchaser and the provider to renegotiate for any excess caseload after a contract limit had been reached. As experience grows of numbers of patients and referrals, DHAs may choose to express their contracts more in terms of 'cost and volume', in preference to block contracts.

Cost per Case

This is a unit price per case, decided in advance, and used as the basis for funding. Here, a hospital is dealing in single numbers and it is appropriate for specialised long-term treatments.

Non-contract Work

A small proportion of hospital work is not covered by contracts. These cases are known as extra-contractual referrals (ECRs). They are of two types: emergency and non-emergency. Emergency treatments have to be paid for by the 'home' DHA, that is where the patient normally resides. Non-emergency treatments have to be approved before treatment commences, so that the provider will be re-imbursed for the cost of treatment by the purchaser, having given prior approval to the course of treatment.

The stages leading to a contract are illustrated in Figure 1.2.

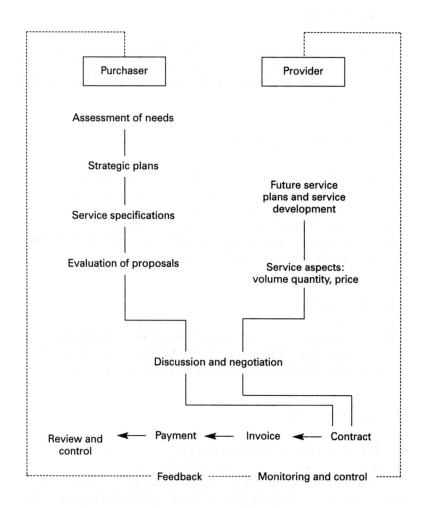

Figure 1.2   Stages leading to a contract

Further Reading

Corry D (ed.) (1997) *Public Expenditure, Effective Management and Control,* The Dryden Press, London.

NHS and Community Care Act 1990. An annual updated summary of changes in health service policy can be found in the *Public Services Yearbook*, published each year by Pitman Publishing, in which there is a Programme Review chapter devoted to health.

Secretaries of State for Health, Social Security, Wales and Scotland (1989), *Caring for People: Community Care in the Next Decade and Beyond*, Cm 849, HMSO, London.

Department of Health (1989) *Working for Patients* Cm 555, DoH, London.

Chapter 2 The Planning and Control of Capital Expenditure: Preparing Capital Estimates

Introduction

In Chapter 1 it was pointed out that the UK government prepared plans for its activities, and differentiated between 'capital' spending and 'current' spending. Capital is a term which is widely used, and indicates that the purpose of the spending is long term: the benefits of acquiring a capital item, such as a health centre, will spread over future years, and the initial cost represents an investment which enables the authority making that investment to continue to function and extend its services. This chapter looks at the way capital spending is planned, co-ordinated, and judged, in the competitive environment of different schemes competing for scarce resources.

Current Expenditure

'Current expenditure' is a term which is used in central government planning; it means the day-to-day expenditure which pays for items such as salaries, wages, supplies, costs of running a service, including office costs, telephones, stationery, and so on.

'Current' is treated separately from 'capital' because traditionally in the planning of governments, current spending represented the on-going commitments and had to be financed each year; capital was more problematic, and needed different considerations.

Planning for Capital

Planning for capital expenditure is usually done at a high level within an organisation, and requires a multidisciplinary approach. The product of planning remains for a long time; for example, district general hospitals may have been planned 20 years ago, or longer: the buildings were planned on the requirements and procedures followed at that time; medical practice will have changed in the intervening period. The length of stay may have shortened due to advances in clinical or diagnostic practice. Care may be outside the hospital, in the community, or under the supervision of the GP, with supporting practice-based staff, rather than hospital-based staff, and consequently the buildings which were 'inherited' may not fully reflect the present needs, work loads, or present day case mix. So many proposals for capital expenditure arise from service needs, to amend, to alter, to adapt buildings. A scheme will probably start as a suggestion from a department, if changes in current practice are needed. Architects or planners will be invited to do a 'space utilisation' survey or report, and some proposals will be made to alter or adapt the layout of the floor, the position of entrances, the siting of partitions, and equipment. Planners will design a number of alternative layouts or solutions, commonly called 'options', and these will be costed. This is not an exercise in precision, but rather an estimate in rough terms of what money might be needed to be set aside to complete the envisaged scheme.

Contract Terms

Some of the terms used at the estimate stage may already be familiar to readers.

Prime Sum

This is a figure to ensure that a particular item is not overlooked, but the figure does not guarantee that the item can be bought for that amount. For example, if a scheme was for building a day room at a hospital, and a TV was required, a prime sum may be included in the estimate showing 'TV £500'. This is to indicate that the actual selection of the set is something which is going to happen at a later date, and it may be regarded as part of the scheme, but at the discretion of the manager involved. Thus, in making the actual purchase, the budget holder may opt for a particular style and size, and the outcome may be that a set is bought for £800, and so the extra £300 would have to be found from some other budget, that is outside the amount provided by or asked for in the capital scheme submission. One way of describing a prime sum is to say it is a 'first guess'.

Provisional Sum

This is an amount which is included in the cost of a scheme, but is a guess, and when the work is actually done, then the true cost will be charged on a basis which has been agreed before-hand in the contract agreement. For example, if a new radio-graphy department was being built, requiring an electricity supply, the work of laying new cable to the site and its entry to the building would probably be estimated in advance, based on the distance the cable had to travel. That calculation would therefore be a 'provisional sum'. When the work was carried out, it is possible that the electricity company would either do the work, or sub-contract it to a contractor, and the work would be charged to the hospital according to a schedule of charges or rates; for example, to cover the different stages of the work; digging out a trench, supplying labour of different skills, hire of machinery, cost of cable, and so on. So the final bill would supersede the 'provisional sum' which had been included in the planning stage, and the final bill may be greater than the 'provisional sum', consequently, some extra finance would be needed. Provisional sums are items which cannot be estimated with accuracy in advance of the work being carried out; and the true cost may be dependent upon factors not known at the time the design stage is being prepared, for example, ground conditions, physical conditions of the site affecting type of foundations, or other imponderables, such as uncertainty about the extent of the work required.

Costing a Capital Scheme

A proposal for a capital scheme will be 'costed', that is money values will be attached to various elements or parts of the work, and, as a result of different skills and techniques being involved, the scheme may appear to be 'owned' by professionals who are outside the department which originated the scheme. So in justifying or presenting the reasons for the scheme, the sponsoring or initiating department will need to be able to explain the different stages and components, and will need to be fully briefed on what has happened to the scheme in all stages of its preparation.

If the scheme is successful in being supported for funding, then it will go forward for inclusion in an annual capital programme. This is an indication that the scheme has satisfied the criteria laid down by the Trust or district authority for inclusion in the programme. Normally, submissions have to be 'standardised' into a particular format for presentation to management and to the policy-making body of the Trust or district authority.

For example, as well as a narrative report which is used to acquaint directors and non-executive members, a table of figures would be prepared to summarise the main elements of cost for which approval was being sought. At the same time, the sponsoring or initiating department would have to indicate the duration of the proposed contract, so that capital finance, the money available to pay for it, could be timed to be raised at the appropriate time to meet the payments. This is known as the 'phasing of capital expenditure payments'.

At the stage of putting these details forward for consideration for inclusion in a capital programme, the department may have to wait its turn until other on-going schemes have been completed, and there is room within the authority's forward plans for a scheme of this size. It is not unusual for a scheme to be approved in principle for inclusion at a later date, when funds allow. What then happens to the figures already prepared which may become out of date due to the passage of time and inflationary pressures on the cost of materials and on wage rates? Generally, a capital expenditure spending proposal is costed out at a certain point in time, and then subsequently the original figures are increased by the use of approved indices which reflect movements in prices. Within the construction industry, architects have access to generally accepted trade price indices, which produce information on a month-by-month basis. When the authority gives the approval for the scheme to go out to tender, a 'bill of quantities' is prepared. In the case of a construction contract, the bill of quantities analyses the requirements in detail, and contractors bidding for the scheme will build up a figure of cost from their own internal knowledge of current prices. The authority or person letting the contract will be able to judge whether the full cost of the contract comes within the amount already envisaged as being the total cost already approved by the authority.

An example of a scheme presented for approval, showing the elements of cost described in the text is shown in Table 2.1.

Schemes of this size will have been controlled by District Health Authorities or by architects contracted to the health authority. They had access to design teams, to specialist advice on planning, and to computer systems to cope with the planning and control of expenditure. Since the health service reforms, district authorities and Trusts follow departmental guidelines relating to capital proposals.

Increasingly, the provision of health care is being influenced by new players in the provision of capital finance. In the 1980s central government channelled some health finance through local authorities, and schemes for joint provision between local councils and district authorities were common. In the 1990s 'Care in the Community' has redefined whole areas of care, and, to meet the different patterns of care, money has been diverted by central government in such a way that agencies and authorities which were previously large participants in schemes have had their role redefined, and others have come on to the scene, with different methods, different approaches, and different financial traditions. Using 'Care of the Elderly' as an example, professional nurses in that area are likely to find an interaction at their level between health care, provided by Trust and hospitals, community care, offered by local authorities through social services, and increasingly more provision by the private sector, through nursing homes, either privately run or through companies. Some developments may be jointly financed, a mixture of publicly funded provision and private investment capital.

Table 2.1   Example of a large capital expenditure proposal

Scheme: Construction of a 40 flat nurses' home at North Hospital

		Phasing of expenditure		
	Total cost £000s	*Year 1 £000s*	*Year 2 £000s*	*Year 3 £000s*
Purchase of site	250	250		
Foundations and site works	120	120		
Construction costs	1,200		800	400
Fitting out				
Internal fittings, equipment	45		45	
Internal services, incl. heating	65			65
Furnishings and furniture	80			80
Total cost estimated at Year 1 prices	**1,760**	**370**	**845**	**545**
If the actual start was delayed three years, then the next report would have the Year 1 figures raised by the effects of price changes e.g. increase in prices and costs between Year 1 and Year 3 is estimated as adding to the cost as follows				
(10 per cent uplift assumed)	176	37	84.5	54.5
Revised total cost	**1,936**	**407**	**929.5**	**599.5**

Interim and Final Certificates for Payments to Contractors

Not all schemes are large ones: clearly, a sponsoring authority has to take great care over the ways in which schemes are put forward, and their physical progress. Much of the work is in the hands of contractors, who require payments as the schemes progress. These are known as 'stage' payments, or 'payments on account', and are based on the completion of certificates, signed by an architect or a quantity surveyor, to indicate that a certain percentage of the total work has been completed. Ultimately, a 'final' certificate is released which grants the balance of the contract monies to the contractor, when all the work covered by the contract has been done to the client's satisfaction. Sometimes, contracts proceed more slowly than expected, or may be completed more quickly than expected. Reasons for delay can include access to the site being delayed by planning enquiries, objections to development, difficult ground conditions, frost or adverse weather, unavailability of components or of specialised equipment. Fast progress can be caused by good weather conditions, good design, in which different trades can work simultaneously instead of waiting for different stages to be completed or the use of integrated components (for example, interior partitions or walls being factory made and incorporating both external finishes and interior wiring for electrics and internal services).

Cash Limits in Capital Schemes

In a situation where an authority has a large capital programme, the finance for it will be determined in advance and usually this is 'cash limited', meaning a fixed sum is available, and no more. So, the monitoring of actual payments made under contracts is vitally important, to ensure that the 'cash limit' is not exceeded. If schemes are temporarily held up, it may be possible to substitute schemes close to the end of the financial year, to use up the available capital finance, and sometimes small schemes are prepared in readiness for what is known as 'slippage' in large schemes. 'Slippage' is where an existing scheme's payments are not going to fall exactly in the year in which they were expected, so there may be a 'shortfall' of payments in one year (for example money not spent as the scheme was not up to date), and when it is completed, there could be an 'excess' or 'overspending' in a following year, when the backlog of payments has to be made, including the shortfall from previous years. For this reason, the best capital programmes are those which include a combination of large and small schemes, and have some in readiness in case remedial action needs to be taken in the last months of a financial year. Sometimes, an authority is accused of having a 'spending spree' in the last months of its financial year, that is February and March, but, upon investigation, these often turn out to be new schemes being placed into the programme to ensure that the allocation of capital money for the year is not lost.

Small Capital Schemes: Example

The criteria for a small scheme may be substantially different from a large scheme. Small schemes usually involve expenditure of £5,000 or more. Ideally, they should offer different ways of providing service in a more cost-effective way; in other words, a small spending of capital should be a forerunner of better conditions, or better outcomes in patient care.

The following is an example of a small capital expenditure proposal, and the way in which it is justified.

The area covered by Health Authority X is 20 miles from north to south, and 12 miles from east to west. Most of the population is concentrated in the central area. In the community services, a doctor is employed to run a clinic on Mondays and Tuesdays in the north, and on Thursdays and Fridays in the south, at two health centres. Wednesdays are spent visiting schools on a rota basis, to hold occasional clinics, but these are very sporadic, and judged not to be totally satisfactory.

As the majority of the referrals to the service come from the centre, they have to travel between eight and ten miles to a clinic: there is no central provision. The doctor's appointments involve the doctor in a fair amount of travelling which is regarded as time wasted.

A capital expenditure proposal has come from the service: adapt a waiting area in one of the central clinics, and use the area so released as a new clinic for the doctor for two days per week (see Table 2.2). One clinic session in the north would be cancelled, leaving the doctor's pattern of attendances as: Monday north; Tuesday and Wednesday central; Thursday and Friday south.

Table 2.2   Example of a small capital expenditure proposal

Capital costs involved	
	£
Building of partitions, new door and walls	4,500
Desk, furniture, and computer	3,200
Decoration and fitting carpets	1,300
Total capital cost	**9,000**

If the scheme went ahead, the authority would not be involved in any additional revenue expenditure. No extra people are being employed as a result of this proposal. The authority would benefit from a reduction in the doctor's travelling expenses. If centrally based for two days, the doctor would not be travelling on those days.

The present budget covers the annual costs of two days in the north clinic: 20-mile round trip for two days times, say, 45 weeks; and two days in the south clinic: 20-mile round trip for two days times, say, 45 weeks.

The new revenue budget would be based on one day in the north clinic (20 miles); two days in the central location with negligible travelling (assuming that the doctor was nominally attached to the central location); and two days in the south as before.

This sort of proposal results in what is known as an 'efficiency saving'. By rearranging the present pattern of provision, and moving the resource (in this case the doctor) to the place where it is needed most (in the central area, where most of the caseload comes from), some costs can be cut out, for example travelling to less than full clinics in the north, and school visits which are regarded as not as effective or as satisfactory as a clinic attendance. The long-term result of this rearrangement is that the potential of the doctor to attend to cases is increased, because more space has been made available by the use of partitions in an existing building, and other space (in the north on Tuesdays) has been released for other purposes.

Efficiency Savings

An 'efficiency saving' is one whereby altering procedures or practice enables more work to be done with fewer resources; in the case of the doctor, the time in the north was not fully accounted for; there was not the demand locally to use up every clinic session: consequently, by moving to the centre, the doctor was able to handle a better flow of cases, and see them closer to their normal location, and not involve them in time spent travelling. With an appointments system, better use could be made of the waiting area releasing room for seeing patients. The annual caseload handled by the doctor was potentially greater under the new system than if the old pattern of clinics had continued.

Is the proposal 'cost effective'? Yes, it appears to be, because the result of altering a central location to house these sorts of referrals has been that the number of cases with appointments each year will be greater than that under the present system. Part of the increase in efficiency is caused by giving the doctor a base out of which to work, instead of travelling to different locations each Wednesday; other efficiencies arise from cutting down the time spent behind the wheel of a car travelling between clinics. The service becomes more effective in the sense that the waiting time for these patients will reduce as more appointments are being made available.

This is an example of a small scheme which has a good chance of being successfully included in a capital programme, for these reasons:

1. It produces greater efficiency, in terms of higher potential throughput of cases, due to the doctor being available at new locations.
2. It is relatively straightforward to implement; no new staff are required.
3. It results in better effectiveness within the service; more clients are reached, without increasing costs, other than small increases in postage and telephones, which would have occurred in the provision of more appointments.

In putting a proposal such as this forward, the main things to remember are these:

1. You need to find out whether this would be regarded as a 'capital' proposal, or a 'revenue' proposal. In this case, as it involves expenditure of over £5,000 in total, it would be classed as 'capital'. Different authorities may, from time to time, adjust the limit for 'capital' expenditure.
2. The scheme needs to be 'costed', that is an estimate of the work requiring to be done, in terms of capital costs.
3. You need to examine and present information on the impact of this proposal on other budget holders, and, in particular, you need to consider the possible consequences of capital expenditure: in this example, there would be savings from other expenditure headings, for example, transport costs, travelling expenses.
4. How far does the proposal fit in with the stated aims of the authority? If, for example, it produces 'efficiency savings', then its case for inclusion in the capital programme will be strengthened.
5. Will it have any 'knock-on effects'? What other aspects of the service may be affected by this change of routine?

Up to this point, small capital schemes have been considered. Many of the considerations in a small scheme apply in the case of a large scheme, but with extra constraints, for example:

- A large scheme may have a long planning period before it becomes fully clear what is required.
- Expenditure may be difficult to justify in competition with other demands from other departments.

● Priorities may be difficult to establish. For example, one department may be seen to be more hard pressed than another, and difficult choices may have to be made by managers and decision makers.

Self-study Questions

1. How would you define 'current expenditure'?
2. What is 'capital expenditure', and where would you find the rules relating to it in your organisation?
3. Distinguish between a 'prime sum' and a 'provisional sum' in a contract.

Further Reading

Allen MW and Myddelton DR (1992) *Essential Management Accounting*, 2nd edn, Prentice Hall, Hemel Hempstead.
Jones R and Pendlebury M (1996) *Public Sector Accounting*, 4th edn, Pitman Publishing, London.

Chapter 3 Methods of Capital Appraisal

Introduction

In Chapter 2 the work of a capital planning team was described, outlining how a multidisciplinary team put together a proposal for a large scheme, having been through the process of identifying needs and priorities. This process culminates in the preparation of a series of reports, some of which are supported by financial information, such as the costs and phasings of money required to pay for the work involved, and an indication of the running costs of any new proposal.

What happens if two or more schemes come forward, and the ability of the authority is limited by cash shortages, and lack of funds? How can you judge the most suitable scheme to go forward in conditions of rationing of available funds?

The solution to this problem may be helped by the use of one or more capital appraisal techniques. The term 'capital appraisal' could be paraphrased and defined as 'the use of a series of tests which results in one scheme becoming more favoured than others on the grounds of its financial attractiveness, assuming that in any final decision the non-financial factors are studied carefully, so that the decision is taken on operational and the service requirements' needs, and that the financial attractiveness of the scheme commends or supports the decision to adopt a particular solution'.

Capital Appraisal

Three different capital appraisal techniques are going to be explained which are widely used in the private sector. They offer assistance in the decision-making process, and ultimately the final decision depends on judgement and sensitivity to service-based issues. The financial techniques are as follows:

1. the accounting rate of return
2. the payback method
3. discounted cash flow (of which there is more than one technique: but the net present value method will be illustrated).

Example using three different project appraisal methods

A hospital Trust in the Midlands is able to spend £100,000 next year on a capital scheme, but is undecided about which of three projects should be undertaken. In all cases, there are sensitive local issues involved, and the Trust wishes to consider the financial implications of each scheme before coming to a final decision.

The costs and expected returns from each project are shown in Table 3.1.

Table 3.1   Costs and expected returns from three capital projects

End of year	Project A	Project B	Project C
Initial outlay Year 0	£100,000	£100,000	£100,000
Cash inflows			
Year 1	10,000	40,000	30,000
2	20,000	35,000	30,000
3	25,000	30,000	30,000
4	30,000	20,000	30,000
5	35,000		25,000
6	35,000		20,000
TOTAL	**155,000**	**125,000**	**165,000**

Project A is an automated car park barrier and video surveillance system on the visitors' car park at the main hospital. Because of local opposition to the idea of making charges for parking at the hospital, their introduction is going to be phased in gradually.

Project B is a scheme to upgrade a conference suite at the hospital, and make it available for outside bookings. It is expected to have a very good initial response, but income may decline from Year 4 onwards due to the opening of a new hotel in close proximity to the hospital, which may attract trade away from the conference suite.

Project C is a refurbishment of bedrooms in nurses' accommodation owned by the Trust, and would result in higher rentals being earned for the improved accommodation.

So, using money as a common measurement in all three projects, it may be possible to compare their respective returns, from the point of view of the Trust. They all cost the same amount of 'capital', that is £100,000, but produce different amounts of revenue to the Trust:

> 'A' brings in £155,000 over six years
> 'B' brings in £125,000 over four years
> 'C' brings in £165,000 over six years

Judging on money values only, Project C seems the best return as it brings in the most. The technique known as the 'accounting rate of return' can be used in situations such as this, to highlight the differences between projects.

So if the Trust wanted to maximise its return on its outlay of £100,000, it would opt for the highest figure (10.8 per cent) and adopt Project C in preference to the other two.

To rank them in order of preference, the results would be:

	Project
First	C
Second	A
Third	B

The figures would be drawn up as shown in Table 3.2.

Table 3.2   Accounting rate of return

	Option 'A' £	Option 'B' £	Option 'C' £
Total amount 'earned' by the scheme	155,000	125,000	165,000
Subtract the initial cost of the scheme	100,000	100,000	100,000
Surplus of income over costs	**55,000**	**25,000**	**65,000**
Divide by the period in years over which this surplus is earned	6 years	4 years	6 years
gives an annual return of	£9,166	£6,250	£10,833
gives an 'annual accounting rate of return' of... on the initial investment of £100,000	9.2%	6.3%	10.8%

The accounting rate of return has a number of practical disadvantages as an appraisal method:

1. It fails to recognise the 'time value of money'. This will be explained later in the chapter when discounting methods are described.
2. It can be adversely affected by different rates of depreciation used by different classes of assets.
3. It can produce the 'wrong' recommendation when compared to other appraisal methods.

Consequently it is of limited use only, and then only if supported by other more reliable methods. It may be used in commercial situations where the rate of return is considered an important element in a capital decision. In the National Health Service the opportunities for its use are very limited, as other more important criteria apply, such as clinical priorities and investment for improved patient care.

The 'Payback Method' of Capital Appraisal

In a situation where capital money is in short supply, the managers of a hospital may feel that one of their priorities is to divert any capital money available into projects which will have a quick return. The illustration of the accounting rate of return depended upon working out the average rate of revenue arising from the project as the criterion for going ahead: the 'payback method' concentrates its attention not on revenues, but on the speed in which the original investment is recovered, on the grounds that, the speedier the return, the more projects can in fact be financed through using the money which returns to the organisation once again.

Using the same figures of cash inflows, that is income arising from each project before charging depreciation, the payback method seeks to determine *when* the flow of revenues equals the amount of the original investment of £100,000. How soon does the original £100,000 come back?

> In project A, it is slightly less than 4½ years
> In B, it is about 2¾ years
> In C, it is 3⅓ years

So, the quickest return is achieved by choosing Project B.
The rankings under the payback method would be:

	Project
First	B
Second	C
Third	A

The following are the main disadvantages of the payback method:

1. It fails to recognise the beneficial effect of positive flows which occur after the payback time, for example, Project C has the biggest return in total, yet comes only second in the ranking, not first.

2. Payback tends to disadvantage projects which move slowly at the outset, but which gain momentum later in terms of earnings.
3. Payback assumes that speed of recovering the original capital investment is more important than other considerations, for example, it tends to ignore the profit potential at the expense of or in preference to the speed of turning over capital.

Discounted Cash Flow Techniques

In general, the use of discounted cash flow techniques is more favoured than either accounting rate of return or payback. Both of these techniques have disadvantages to the operational manager.

Discounting brings into the consideration of options the time value of money. This is a way of recognising that the flow of money in the future will be influenced by matters such as the passage of time, and the method seeks to recognise this in its assumptions and methodology.

What is the time effect of money? The project is assumed to be built in a 'year of outlay', known as Year 0.

Cash inflows are expected at the end of each subsequent year: 12 months after Year 0, we have the first revenue arising, called Year 1. Revenue is assumed to come in on the final day of that year; the next year's revenue comes in at Year 2, again, on the final day of that year.

The profile of spending and receipts is shown in Table 3.3.

Table 3.3 Spending and receipts profile

Year 0	Year 1	Year 2
Initial outlay or investment in the project	First money or income received	Second amount of money received

The technique of 'discounting' looks at the amounts and timing of future cash flows, and expresses them in terms of the start of the project. Does the future revenue justify the investment at the beginning? How do we bring future revenues into the reckoning? Basically, future money is estimated at the time it occurs, then is expressed as a figure which if invested at the start of the project at a known rate of interest, would produce the actual amount of revenue expected at the specified future date. Most management accounting texts and some computer software products contain the mathematical figures you need for such a calculation.

Example of Net Present Value

If we assume that an organisation can borrow money at a cost of 10 per cent per annum, we can use discounting tables to decide whether any capital expenditure proposal is worthwhile. The discounting factors which we need will be described in the tables or software as 'present value figures of £1 received after a period of years at 10 per cent'.

The factors for 10 per cent are as follows:

After 1 year	.9091
2 years	.8264
3 years	.7513

So, assuming that you made an investment of £2,400 in Year 0, and it produced £1,000 income in each of three successive years, and the cost of borrowing money to your organisation was 10 per cent per annum, would the investment produce sufficient revenue to justify the initial outlay?

Method: Show the original outlay in Year 0

Year 0   £2,400

Then record the revenue received in each year

Income Year 1   £1,000
Year 2   £1,000
Year 3   £1,000

Apply the appropriate discount factor from tables, in this case the cost of capital to the organisation is 10 per cent, so the 10 per cent factor would be used (see Table 3.4).

Table 3.4   Net present value

Year	Revenue	Factor @ 10%	Multiply revenue by the factor
Year 1	£1,000	.9091	£909
Year 2	£1,000	.8264	£826
Year 3	£1,000	.7513	£751
Total discounted revenue is			£2,486
Subtract the value of the initial outlay			£2,400
which leaves a positive residual amount of			£86

Provided the residual amount at the end of the project's life is positive, then the project is worth proceeding with, and is worth supporting as it covers its cost and the cost of borrowing the capital to undertake it. If the final result is negative, then the revenues do not justify the outlay involved.

The use of discounting methods, such as discounted cash flow, is regarded as being more sophisticated than other methods of capital appraisal, such as the accounting rate of return and the payback method.

The element of sophistication comes from the fact that discounting takes into consideration the life of a project over a specified period of time, and takes into account the time value of money, that is, the fact that money becomes eroded in its purchasing power over the passage of time. For that reason, discounting methods are preferable to the accounting rate of return method, or the payback method, as neither of these allows for the time value of money.

In preparing a mathematical approach to a problem, you should remember the basic assumptions, and make these clear to people using the appraisal as a basis for decision making. Some things are not capable of being measured in terms of money, such as efficiency savings, or saving in waiting time, or reduction in the length of waiting lists, and these items need to be mentioned alongside the financial results of appraisals, so that the non-financial elements of a decision are apparent as well as the financial information.

Returning to the appraisal for Projects A, B, and C, we can use discounted cash flow or net present value techniques. Assume in this situation that the cost of capital required to finance this scheme would be 12 per cent per annum, so a factor of 12 per cent would be used (see Table 3.5).

Table 3.5 Calculations of the discounted value (net present value)

Factor at 12% Revenue A £	Discounted value £	Revenue B £	Discounted value £	Revenue C £	Discounted value £
.8929 10,000	8,929	40,000	35,716	30,000	26,787
.7929 20,000	15,858	35,000	27,752	30,000	23,787
.7118 25,000	17,795	30,000	21,354	30,000	21,354
.6355 30,000	19,065	20,000	12,710	30,000	19,065
.5674 35,000	19,859			25,000	14,185
.5066 35,000	17,731			20,000	10,132
	99,237		97,532		115,310
Deduct initial outlay of	100,000		100,000		100,000
Result	**–(763)**		**–(2,468)**		**15,310**
	Negative		**Negative**		**Positive (this would be the preferred option)**

Under the accounting rate of return method C came out best.

Under payback, the results favoured B as it had the quickest return of the original investment.

Under discounting methods, the rating was

	Project
First	C
Second	A
Third	B

Discounting methods seem to be the most suitable for capital appraisal, and match more closely than the other methods the commercial considerations of those whose capital is at risk. They have been used in the health service for the appraisal of capital projects, and proposals usually adopt a 'test discount rate' which is specified in Department of Health guidelines. The test discount rate is a specified rate of interest as recommended at the time by the Treasury in view of current interest rate conditions and it is used to compare the effect of mutually exclusive projects. In the private sector, the opportunity cost of capital is substituted for the test discount rate.

Capital proposals therefore represent an important part of preparing for the future development of services. The steps described in this chapter have emphasised that the initial stages are ones of close co-operation between different professionals: the capital proposal becomes multifaceted; the reports which describe its adoption need to be informative, and should be based on a careful consideration of all the options available.

The mathematics or accounting associated with such proposals is not too difficult; but, there are circumstances where some techniques are not appropriate, and the user needs to be aware of the limitations inherent in some of the techniques used.

Self-study Questions

1. What is slippage in a capital contract?
2. How useful is the payback method of capital appraisal and what are its disadvantages over other methods?
3. Describe the use of the accounting rate of return as a guide to capital investment.

4. What are the benefits of using discounted cash flow (net present value) in a capital appraisal compared with other techniques (for example payback)?

Further Reading

Allen MW and Myddelton DR (1992) *Essential Management Accounting*, 2nd edn, Prentice Hall, Hemel Hempstead.

Davies DB (1997) *The Art of Managing Finance*, 3rd edn, McGraw-Hill, Maidenhead.

Holmes P (1998) *Investment Appraisal*, International Thomson Business Press, London.

Mott G (1993) *Investment Appraisal*, M and E Handbook Series, 2nd edn, Pitman Publishing, London.

Chapter 4 Sources of Capital Finance – Paying for Capital Expenditure Schemes and Capital Allocation

Introduction

This chapter examines some of the sources of capital available to the National Health Service. It also looks at some of the alternative ways of providing finance for capital projects.

Sources of Funds

Unconditional or Block Capital

Each year NHS Trusts and health authorities are notified of a sum of capital money which they are able to spend on their own schemes. In the case of NHS Trusts this is done via the external financing limit (EFL) and in the case of health authorities via an allocation of resources.

The main aim behind unconditional capital is that it should be used to maintain the NHS asset base. The amount each Trust receives is determined by reference to the turnover of the Trust and the depreciation value of the assets. However, it is not a uniform approach across the country and the regional offices of the NHS Executive are allowed discretion in how they apply the formula.

The sorts of item that the money will be spent on include:

- replacement medical equipment
- information technology
- health and safety
- major maintenance of building and plant.

Inevitably, some Trusts will choose to buy new things with the money but a balance must be kept between maintaining existing services and assets and developing new ones. With medical equipment it is also true that replacement items will include new and improved technology.

The process by which each Trust decides what the money will be spent on will vary but typically there may be sub-groups to look at each of the major headings. Departments within the Trust will be asked to submit bids to meet their own requirements. These bids will almost certainly exceed the money available and some system of prioritisation will be needed. This is particularly important in respect of any purchases, particularly of equipment, to ensure that there is no financial penalty to be incurred if a piece of equipment is replaced before the end of its useful life. Taking a vehicle as an example, if you replace your own car before you have paid off the loan you will still have the financial consequences of the balance of the loan to pay off. The same is true of any outstanding depreciation on assets which remain as a cost in the books of Trusts.

Conditional or Discretionary Capital

In addition to the annual sum of unconditional capital, Trusts and health authorities will have the opportunity to bid the NHS Executive regional offices for additional sums of money for large new capital projects or for schemes which exceed their delegated limit. Such bids will need to be supported by a business case, which is a detailed document setting out the service and financial issues and containing an option appraisal of the proposed investment.

The level of delegation is determined by reference to the turnover of the Trust. Schemes with a value above the delegated limit have to be submitted for approval.

For NHS Trusts the sums involved are likely to exceed their internal resources to fund such schemes and therefore Trusts will be allowed to borrow funds to finance the scheme if it is to be financed from public funds. The money will then be repaid over a period of time in the form of a loan. An alternative (discussed in the next section) is to explore the options for private finance.

Private Finance

The Private Finance Initiative (PFI) was first introduced under the Conservative government in the early 1990s. From 1997, under the Labour government, PFI is subject to a major review and is now being viewed as a Public Private Partnership (PPP).

The aim of PFI/PPP is to attract private sector money to fund public sector projects for which the private sector will attract an income stream. The emphasis to date in the NHS has been on large capital schemes, for example new hospitals but the NHS has encountered significant difficulties in bringing them to a conclusion mainly because of concerns around the powers of NHS Trusts to enter into such schemes and the long-term future prospects in a rapidly changing environment such as the NHS.

A number of smaller schemes have been successful, for example retail developments on hospital sites, car parking, catering.

Leasing/Facilities Management

An alternative to outright purchase particularly of equipment and information technology is to look at some form of facilities management. This generally seeks to avoid paying out large one-off sums of capital by spreading the cost of a project over several years. Such a scheme must demonstrate value for money and certain financial criteria must be met, for example the Trust must ensure that it has an annual revenue stream to meet the cost of the lease which is likely to be an operating lease.

Facilities management may go one step further in that in addition to spreading the cost of equipment over a period of time, a private company may also take over the running of a particular function of the Trust, for example the information technology department.

Further Reading

Department of Health (1996) *Capital Allocation – Summary Paper*, DoH, London.
Health Literature Line 0800 555 777

Chapter 5 The Planning and Control of Revenue Expenditure

In the corridors of Westminster, the government's annual budget attracts a lot of press and media attention, culminating in the annual event when members of Parliament crowd into the Chamber of the House of Commons to hear the Chancellor's statement. This is usually televised, with comments from observers on the general economic climate and the measures proposed by the Chancellor to reshape or reframe the economy during the next 12 months. The process which the government of the day goes through is one of review of existing activities, and of negotiation, in following through the proposals of spending departments and agreeing in total a funding package to allow departments to carry out their objectives.

In terms of centrally organised activities, the government has aims and responsibilities, conferred by statute, and these general aims, such as the 'defence of the realm', the 'education of children of compulsory school age' or the 'maintenance of a system of health provision for all ages, irrespective of income or means' are then divided up into specific responsibilities and expressed as objectives, which are taken on board or absorbed within the objectives of a provider of that service, to the extent that the provider can fund, finance or pay for the provision of that care.

Just as central government has to plan ahead, so too have agencies and deliverers of service in the public and the private sector. The public sector has a long tradition and background of budgeting methods; originally, the amount of taxation which was made available to the public sector to carry out its functions was limited, and central government has to 'ration' the amount of cash being released to spenders. This process of rationing or of sharing out the available funds between different competing services was known as 'resource allocation'. In the health service, there was a Resource Allocation Working Party which was made up of senior officers of regional and district authorities, and they examined a whole series of indicators of the state of health of the nation, and related this to statistical and census information, in such a way that the available money nationally was redistributed by the Department of Health in fairness to known conditions within the population. At the end of this annual exercise, a district finance office or director of finance would have an indication of how much money was being made available on which to run the local services for the next 12 months.

Thus, a revenue allocation is a cash-limited sum at district level for on-going expenditure. 'Cash limited' means that it represents a ceiling; extra funding is not likely to be available after the notification has been made, so authorities are obliged to keep within their notified figure of resources.

The annual settlement or determination of the funds for revenue purposes therefore represents an important constraint on the activities of health authorities. They have to go through an annual planning exercise, in the same manner as the central government, to ensure that their policy aims, translated into objectives and into programmes will be achievable within the levels of finance which have been authorised or agreed in advance.

There are a number of ways in which revenue funds can be controlled, and different methods have been used from time to time. The main styles or methods of control are now described.

Incrementalism

Widely used, this consists of taking last year's budgeted spending, and increasing it by an across-the-board percentage of extra funds, and allowing everything to proceed into a new year without a major review. In essence, those organisations which opt for an incremental approach are doing so because they believe that the great bulk of their work is continuous or on-going from year to year, and that a percentage increase of funding to cope with the known effects of pay awards and price increases will achieve the same level of service in a future year. If you operate on an incremental basis, then the mathematics is fairly simple: you know the current year's level of costs, and you can assume that there will be a percentage increase added on for next year. The extra money may be at a different rate for pay items, for example a nurses' pay award at a certain percentage rate, than for non-pay items, such as drugs, consumable items, furniture, equipment, and so on. But is a percentage approach fair? What happens if next year's allowance is not sufficient to cover the actual costs encountered in that year?

Suppose each year you are funded to buy four new beds on a large ward, to replace ones which are no longer suitable. Suppose the basic budget is £800 per bed, plus an allowance for price rises of 5 per cent, giving £840 per bed as the amount available. If the price from the manufacturer is £880 each, the manufacturer's price increase of 10 per cent per bed has not been matched by the hospital's allowance for inflation, which was 5 per cent. The dilemma then is do you buy three beds, and keep within budget, or do you place an order for four beds, and in doing so, exceed your budget allowance, and overspend? Overspending is generally taken as an indication of poor management. If you underspend and only buy three, you could also be accused of poor management, as the ward would have had four beds out of service, and replacements available for only three.

Consequently, incrementalism may be fine in allocating out extra money, as a means of distributing resources, but it may cause problems of under- and overspending. It needs to be refined, and there are various methods of doing this.

Line–item Budgeting

This is an approach which groups together a range of similar items and controls the total spending of the heading, that is the line in the budget, instead of controlling the components one by one. For example, in the case of the four beds used earlier, the budget may include them in a heading such as 'ward equipment renewals', and as long as the total for ward equipment was not exceeded over a period of a year, the budget holder could still have four beds, even at an inflated price, if other items which were not such a priority were held back, and the money for them was not spent. Thus an overspending of £160 on the purchase of four beds would not be reported or conspicuous because somewhere in the same year a similar amount could be saved by not spending on an item which was within the same budget heading. A budget holder needs to be aware of the total value of the budget and ensure that the maximum allowed is not exceeded. This is good housekeeping in practice.

Virement

This is a French word meaning a 'transfer of money' from one heading to another. In the public sector virement is an indication that money has been switched, and although extra money has been spent, the effect overall is that the total budget has not been exceeded. The word is used when, for example, delays may have occurred which prevent money being spent, and that money is switched, or vired, to another heading, which can then go ahead and buy at a faster rate than originally planned. In total, within the confines of a year, the global previously 'approved' total is not exceeded.

Example of Virement

A health district is planning to buy a vehicle for taking a mobile display to schools to show children the effects of neglecting their teeth, and the consequences of poor diet. The original budget is shown in Table 5.1.

Table 5.1   Dental education: original budget

Dental education in schools initiative	
	£
Driver's wages and National Insurance	11,200
Publicity and promotional material	5,100
Vehicle running expenses	
Petrol, oil and servicing	400
Licensing	126
Total	**16,826**

Let us suppose that the vehicle was a four-wheel drive specialised one, and that there was a six-month waiting period between order and delivery.

If it was ordered on 1 April, the start of the financial year, the earliest it would be ready would be 1 October. There would, therefore, be no point in employing a driver until 1 October at the earliest.

So the manager in charge of health education in schools could apply for 'virement'. This releases money voted or authorised for one purpose, and transfers it to another heading, with the overall result that work of a different type is undertaken, and financially the organisation is not overspending. In this example, the manager could use the non-availability of the vehicle to move further ahead on a different type of promotion, for example to move money from the 'employees' heading of 'driver's wages and National Insurance' and transfer it to 'publicity and promotional expenditure'. A short report would have to be drawn up to describe the circumstances of the request for virement, and to identify the proposed new expenditure.

Table 5.2   Dental education: budget report

Example of report

The original budget was prepared on the basis that the initiative for dental education was to run for a full year. Due to delays between the ordering and delivery of the vehicle, the original budget will not be needed in full, and it is proposed to bring forward a different programme, using the expenditure originally provided in the Schools Initiative. A display of materials relating to the new programme will be on display at the meeting of the Management Board.

Dental education in schools initiative

	Original budget	Now proposed	Amount of change
	£	£	£
Driver's wages and National Insurance	11,200	5,600	–5,600
Publicity and promotional material	5,100	10,963	+5,863
Vehicle running expenses			
Petrol, oil and servicing	400	200	–200
Licensing	126	63	–63
	16,826	**16,826**	**nil**

In this example, six months' spending on wages and related costs, and on petrol and licensing, has been saved by the vehicle not being available, and the manager or budget holder is putting forward a request for the money saved to be transferred to another heading, with the overall result that the total spending will not exceed the amount previously approved. This is virement, and usually applications like this are given the go-ahead providing that:

1. The saving is fortuitous, that is, it came about by conditions outside the authority's control, and was not planned to be like this. If it is a genuine saving, then it is not a back door method of paying for expenditure which was not likely to succeed in any other way.
2. The 'new' expenditure proposal is not likely to pre-empt future resources, for example an authority or a Trust would not normally approve spending on staff-related matters, as additional staff voted or approved through virement could in effect be a continuing commitment beyond the end of the period in which the fortuitous saving was made. That would have an inflationary effect, as it would be extra, continuing expenditure in the future.

Supplementary Votes or Supplementary Expenditure

The system of supplementary approvals of expenditure is used in conjunction with incremental budgeting. This allows an authority to grant an increase to a budget heading at a later date to the main budget approval, and usually as a result of extra funding becoming available. It differs from virement, as in virement no new levels of expenditure are envisaged, whereas in a supplementary situation, there is a clear acknowledgement that extra spending is being authorised.

Advantages and Disadvantages of Incrementalism

Looking at things from a total point of view, an incremental approach to budgeting has its adherents. In its favour, you can say that if last year's money was adequate to run a service, then a new approval of 'last year's money + a percentage for inflation and growth' should be a fairly easily understandable way of sharing out resources. You then concentrate each year on deciding what is an adequate measure for 'inflation', that is pay and price increases, and what is fair in total terms for 'growth', or 'new' service. However, there will be many competing claims for new 'growth' money: how does the manager handle the selection procedure, and the 'weeding out' of unsuitable bids? One way is to consider the new money in isolation: to regard it as a fund out of which new activities will be paid, and consider them as 'authority-supported initiatives' rather than departmental initiatives. If the total new money is restricted, then it makes more sense to prioritise and attach the money to those schemes which have a high profile and a high degree of support. As a consequence, some departments may receive extra funding which is disproportionately high compared with what they would have been entitled to if the available new growth money was allocated or shared out on the basis of a percentage of existing expenditure.

Thus, incrementalism focuses attention on the margins. It takes as uncontroversial the broad mass of expenditure, and primarily concentrates decision-makers' attention upon marginal changes. In doing so, we have to consider equality, fairness, equity, and future burdens on the service. Expansion of a service through extra revenue money is bound to be a contentious issue; managers who feel they have had their claims or 'bids' rejected will feel demotivated. To counter this, the trend in recent years has been to supplement the 'new money' fund by taking money from elsewhere to supplement the amounts available for expansion. For example, the principle of 'top slicing' is now fairly commonplace. This 'creams off' some of the money for ordinary revenue purposes, and adds it to the new money, so that some of the priority schemes can go ahead sooner than if they waited their turn and were totally reliant on new money only. With top slicing you are effectively taking money out of the existing revenue budget, and transferring it to the 'new growth' total. If the ordinary revenue funds are reduced in this way, there will be less money available to do the same volume of work, and health service managers are acquainted with this practice, and with the terminology which accompanies it, that of making 'efficiency savings'.

So with incrementalism: there are strong supporters of it, on the grounds that it runs from year to year without major disturbance, and is relatively consistent in its operation. Others may feel that it is too vague when coming down to a unit or ward level, and the way it operates, using percentage increases, is not sufficiently precise for day-to-day control of departmental or clinical specialty budgets. The broad majority of authorities operate an incremental system, and safeguard against deficiencies in the system through a range of measures:

1. A set of standing financial instructions or financial regulations define the framework within which budget holders and the authority or Trust will operate.
2. Annual budgets are analysed into convenient shorter periods, so that spending against budget can be monitored before overspending becomes an issue.
3. Other controls are inserted, which reinforce the ability of the budget to become a useful control and feedback mechanism, for example staff numbers and staff availability is monitored through personnel departments and by operational staff, such as directors of nursing services. Not only is the cost of staff a consideration in keeping within budget, but staff mix or skill mix are equally important at ward level.
4. Computer software and systems support is needed to translate budgets which have been compiled on an incremental basis into workable and controllable management units. Ideally, budgets should cascade down an organisation so that the sum of the parts equals the total budget. Clearly, there are difficulties in sharing out some costs, especially those relating to central departments, but providing the treatment is consistent between years, and providing there is a willingness to operate as close to the budget as possible, then the budget can be a useful tool to a manager who wishes to either expand or maintain the service, as figures produced from previous periods will support the case made for expansion or extensions of service.

Zero-based Budgeting

This is an approach which is different again from incrementalism. It is an attempt to set up a forecast of what will be needed to run a service or a department, where everything is considered in detail from a starting point of having to justify every item of expenditure. It is known by its initials, ZBB. Clearly, the amount of time and effort required makes it impracticable for widespread application, for example, it would take years of work to transfer an organisation which had been running on incremental lines to a zero base. However, the technique and the procedures of zero-based budgeting are especially suitable for new situations, and managers are often forced to take a service and establish a budget for the first time. The main advantages of building a budget in this way are that it avoids the perpetuation of 'obsolete' expenditure, and it makes available a record of decisions taken and the reasons for them.

This should improve the quality of decision taking, and will monitor situations as they develop. Unexpected events which happen in the course of an operational situation will be highlighted, and after discussion, can be incorporated into the future budget planning. Zero-based budgets are therefore responsive to developments, and are less rigid than an incremental approach.

Most authorities and Trusts operate incremental budgeting on the vast majority of their activities, on the grounds that this technique mirrors national conditions and can be refined according to national pronouncements or changes in funding. They may also use a zero-based approach to a more limited extent where new proposals are coming on-stream for the first time, and the outcome of zero-based budgeting is that a separate reporting mechanism is set up which, when it has established a stability of its own, can be incorporated into the incremental base of the whole authority or the Trust.

Self-study Questions

1. How would you define a cash limit in relation to a budget?
2. How would you explain virement in the context of a health service budget?
3. Describe the main features of incrementalism and contrast it with a zero-based approach to budgeting.

Further Reading

Allen MW and Myddleton DR (1992) *Essential Management Accounting,* 2nd edn, Prentice Hall, Hemel Hempstead.

Glynn JJ, Perrin J and Murphy MP (1994) *Accounting for Managers,* Chapman & Hall, London.

Jones R and Pendlebury M (1996) *Public Sector Accounting,* 4th edn, Pitman Publishing, London.

Mellett H, Marriott N and Harries S (1993) *Financial Management in the NHS: A Manager's Handbook,* Chapman & Hall, London.

Chapter 6 Setting a Budget for the First Time

Introduction

The purpose of this section is to examine the methods of setting a budget for the first time. It represents the ideal opportunity to get it right first time as it is unlikely there will be much opportunity to revisit the budget at a later date. The approach will vary according to the scale of the scheme but the same principles will apply whether it is a small or large project.

Types of Cost

The costs likely to be incurred fall into various categories:

1. direct, indirect, overheads
2. fixed, semi-fixed, variable
3. recurrent, non-recurrent.

Direct Costs–Staffing

These are the costs which will be incurred at the point of delivery of the scheme or service. The main element in the NHS will be staffing.

The key to ensuring the correct level of finance for staffing is to ensure that the numbers, grade and skill mix are accurate. It is then relatively simple to apply the costs.

The information for determining the appropriate staffing levels can be obtained from a range of sources:

1. comparison with existing similar schemes in the organisation
2. comparison with existing similar schemes in other organisations
3. professional judgement
4. use of norms or benchmarking comparisons.

The staffing mix will need to take account of:

1. the working arrangements, for example five or seven day, 9 am–5 pm or 24 hours
2. the workflow – is it busier in the mornings or afternoons or is it constant? Are there any seasonal fluctuations, for example winter/summer variations?
3. the workload and intensity of work.

The cost will need to take account of:

- sickness/absence levels
- enhancements to working conditions, for example night duty, weekend duty.

To actually arrive at a cost, various approaches may be used:

1. Staff in the NHS are usually employed on an incremental scale, that is the salary automatically increases each year for a period of 4–5 years until staff reach the maximum of the scale. Therefore in calculating the cost should it be based on the minimum, mid-point, mean or maximum of the scale? This is illustrated as follows:

$$£$$

Scale point 1 – 15,000
Scale point 2 – 15,750
Scale point 3 – 16,300
Scale point 4 – 16,650
Scale point 5 – 17,000

Therefore:

- the minimum is   £15,000
- the mid-point is   £16,300
- the mean is   £16,000 (that is, the average between the minimum and maximum)
- the maximum is   £17,000.

Normal practice is to use the mid-point which works on the principle that there will be a reasonable turnover of staff and at any time some will be on the minimum and some on the maximum. However, the labour market has in the last few years tended to be reasonably static and it may be more prudent to cost everything at the maximum.

2. To the basic salary costs will need to be added the costs of employment or 'on-costs'. These are employers' National Insurance and employers' superannuation or pension contributions. There is no addition for employees' contributions as these are included in the basic salary costs.

3. There are two elements of enhancements to be considered:

- When staff are on holiday or off sick the work still needs to be undertaken and replacement staff will be needed in most cases. The holidays can easily be determined, the more difficult calculation is in making an assessment of how much sickness an employee may have. The usual practice is to add a percentage uplift to the cost of the basic salary.
- The second element under the heading of enhancements involves the additional cost of staff working nights and/or weekends depending on the type of service. The cost will be derived from analysing the rota that staff are required to work. For example staff might be entitled to time and a half or double time or the basic salary.

Direct Costs – Non-staffing

Using the approaches described earlier, for example comparison with other schemes/organisations/benchmarking, a similar process will need to be followed for non-pay. The main problem with non-pay is that it is very easy to forget something, in particular where it is another department that is responsible for providing the service. A very simple process to adopt is to have a standard list of all non-pay costs and to mark those that apply to your budget.

These might be classed into:

1. those that come under your direct control
2. those that are provided by other departments.

Examples under category 1 might include:

- drugs
- dressings.

Examples under category 2 might include:

- pathology
- cleaning
- radiology
- heating.

The split very much depends on the service that is being established. The key to identifying the correct cost is to ensure that the service is clearly defined so that all concerned can calculate the costs involved.

Indirect Costs

There will also be a range of costs which will not impact directly on the budget that is being established but where the service will be expected to contribute to the overall costs of the organisation. Examples could include finance or personnel. It may be that in the final analysis these departments are able to absorb the extra work but it is important to include them at the outset. It is far easier to take costs out at the beginning than to add them in at a later date.

Another way of analysing the cost is under the heading of fixed, semi-fixed and variable. As a simple equation:

$$
\begin{array}{ccc}
\text{Direct} & & \text{Fixed} \\
+ & = & + \\
\text{Indirect} & & \text{Semi-fixed} \\
+ & & + \\
\text{Overheads} & & \text{Variable}
\end{array}
$$

The costs overall are the same but the treatment of the items can provide a different perspective particularly once the service is up and running.

Fixed

Fixed costs will remain unchanged irrespective of the level of service that is provided, for example whether you treat one patient or ten patients the cost is the same. Examples include rates, senior management costs.

Semi-fixed

Semi-fixed costs will change as activity changes but only at given intervals for example 1–20 patients, 20–40 patients. Other examples include staffing costs, which are particularly crucial when setting staffing levels, and cleaning arrangements.

Variable

Variable costs will change as each individual patient is treated. Examples include drugs and dressings.

Telephones provide a useful example of both a fixed and a variable cost. The rental will be fixed because irrespective of the number of calls the rental is the same. However, the call charge will be variable as it will be totally dependent on the number of calls made.

The analysis under the headings of fixed, semi-fixed and variable can be particularly important if a service is to be introduced in stages and also for monitoring purposes once the service is up and running.

Recurrent/non-recurrent

Terminology that is often used in the NHS refers to costs (and funding) that is recurrent or non-recurrent.

Recurrent costs are those that occur year on year.

Non-recurrent are those that occur only once. These can often relate to costs incurred in the set-up of a new service.

Self-study Questions

1. Distinguish between what is meant by mid-point and mean in the context of salary scales
2. Indicate some of the on-costs which are usually associated with salaries' estimates
3. Distinguish between fixed, semi-variable and variable costs and give health service examples for each category of cost.

Further Reading

Mellett H, Marriott N and Harries S (1993) *Financial Management in the NHS: A Manager's Handbook*, Chapman & Hall, London.

Chapter 7 Monitoring of Budget Performance

Introduction

The purpose of this chapter is to examine the process for monitoring budget performance and to examine cost behav
iour, exception reporting and ways of dealing with under-
and overspendings.

Budget Monitoring

Budget monitoring in the NHS, and indeed most organisations,
takes place over a 12-month time frame with month-by-month
analysis of performance. A typical budget statement will have a
series of headings such as:

- annual budget
- monthly budget
- monthly expenditure
- monthly variance
- cumulative budget
- cumulative expenditure
- cumulative variance to date.

In addition there will also be information on staffing typically:

- funded establishment
- actual establishment.

The budget statement will form the basis for determining a range of issues, in particular whether there is a need to take corrective action and what form of action that will entail.

One important feature of the budget statement is that it should confirm simply what the budget holder should already know. Any variances should not come as a surprise. However, in reality the budget statement is often the first indicator that everything is either alright or that there are problems.

It is equally important to understand not only why a budget may be overspent but also why it is underspent.

Analysing the Budget

Typically a budget statement will be produced as soon as possible after the end of the month to which it refers. The aim should be no later than ten working days.

The immediate focus will be on the overall position but it will be necessary to check the movements on individual budget lines to ensure that there is nothing untoward. It is the responsibility of each budget holder to undertake this review.

Individual budget statements will be amalgamated to produce the summary position for a directorate. This will normally be accompanied by a written report from the accountant (directorate accountant/financial advisor) highlighting key points.

As mentioned earlier, it is important that underspendings are looked at just as closely as overspendings for example:

1. Has something been missed?
2. Has expenditure been incurred which relates to future months?
3. Was the budget holder expecting expenditure to be incurred? Has an assessment been made if the invoice has not been paid?

Overall the budget holders need to satisfy themselves that the position accurately reflects the position of their department.

Phasing the Budget

A common problem in the NHS is the extent to which a budget should be phased in line with anticipated expenditure. Simply to take your annual budget and divide it by 12 which does not reflect the expenditure pattern could result in incorrect decisions being taken.

Some simple examples are:

1. There is a greater volume of medical cases in the winter than the summer.
2. Energy costs will be higher in the winter than the summer.
3. Drugs are issued daily to patients. Therefore, minor changes should be made for 30- and 31-day months.
4. Bank holidays will result in higher salaries and wages costs because of enhanced payment rates.

Terminology

Terminology can sometimes be difficult to interpret. An over-spending may be indicated by:

1. a + in front of the variance
2. adverse/unfavourable/bad.

An underspending may be indicated by:

1. a – in front of the variance
2. favourable/good
3. brackets ( ) around the figures.

Taking Action

Any course of action will be determined by the reason for the over- or underspending. The action itself is likely to take time to have an effect. By the time that the position has been validated as correct and appropriate analysis undertaken, three to four weeks may have elapsed.

The decision on what action to take may require senior authorisation. Also, given that the majority of expenditure in the NHS is staffing, changes to staffing levels could again take time to implement. The view has to be taken as to whether the action is permanent or temporary.

It is important, therefore, seriously to consider whether the action proposed will, in the time available, correct the budgetary position. This can be very difficult to achieve if such a situation arises late in the financial year, and may mean that additional short-term measures are required to correct any in-year issues.

If there is likely to be an underspending, it is also important to identify this early so that decisions can be taken as to whether to use the money for something else, or to leave it as an underspending to offset an overspending elsewhere in the organisation.

Further Reading

Glynn JJ, Perrin J and Murphy MP (1995) *Accounting for Managers*, Chapman & Hall, London.

Mellett H, Marriott N and Harries S (1993) *Financial Management in the NHS: A Manager's Handbook*, Chapman & Hall, London.

Wilson RMS and McHugh G (1996) *Financial Analysis: A Managerial Introduction*, Cassell, London.

Chapter 8 Putting it all Together

Introduction

One of the features of the health service is that the whole activity within a hospital is geared towards keeping within budget, and that the total spending is made up of adding together all the small budgets. Understanding the organisational structure is important. This chapter outlines how the structure of the hospital is reflected in the financial information on which important decisions and switches of resources are made.

Organisational Structures

Under the Resource Management Initiative (1991), hospitals were divisionalised, and the idea which had been developed during the 1980s of adopting a specialty approach was formalised by the creation of *directorates*. Each manager of a directorate is supported by a nurse manager and a business manager. Thus, if a hospital had a specialty of for example, ear, nose and throat (ENT), the directorate or management team of that directorate would be a consultant or doctor, as head of the directorate, a nurse manager, and a business manager. The way in which a hospital divides up its specialties into directorates will determine the organisational structure of the hospital, and the budgeting will be a natural consequence, flowing from the pre-determined organisational arrangements. Organisational structure is shown in Figure 8.1.

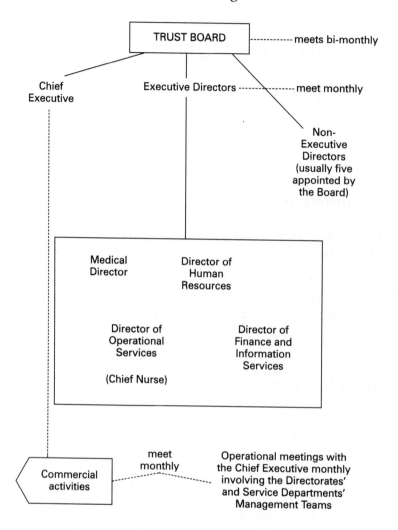

Figure 8.1   Organisational structure of a large acute hospital

The Challenge

Assuming that a hospital has divided itself into directorates, the challenge then comes of containing expenditure within the expected levels of income. The reason we have financial information is to enable managers to monitor spending and to take corrective action if preliminary indications reveal that over-spending is likely.

How are Budgets Determined?

The income which a Trust receives is largely as a result of negotiated contracts, as explained in Chapter 1. The total possible or estimated income is known in advance. The task of the directorates is to prepare their own expenditure budgets in such a way that the totality of expenditure is within the income estimate. Table 8.1 shows a sample summary of income and expenditure.

Some departments have no income. Radiography acts as a support service for the rest of the hospital, and in such cases, an equitable way has to be found of sharing the cost of that department among the departments which have use of its services, so that in effect radiography has a notional income which is derived from recharges to other departments or directorates.

So the task of determining the budget starts by estimating the expected level of activity within a directorate for a future 12-month period, and calculating how much that level of activity will cost. As a starting point, one might take the approved spending plans of last year, and add on any development money which has been secured, and an allowance for levels of inflation, covering an estimate of increases in pay and prices affecting the service, and then the total expenditure estimate is the sum of three things: last year, development and inflation. Table 8.2 shows a sample ward budget.

The total costs are then linked to the level of activity, for example, to arrive at indicators of possible costs for clinical intervention (for example, costs per consultant day, costs of a particular procedure, or output such as in-patient days) and if the costs are in line with the agreed levels of funding, the directorate's budget is approved.

Table 8.1 Summary of income and expenditure for a large acute hospital

	General surgery £	General medical £	Children's services £	Obstetrics and gynaecology £	Ear, nose and throat £	Radiology £	Pathology £	Pharmacy £	Theatres £	Support services £
Income										
Block contract income										
Extra contract referrals										
General practitioner fundholders										
Private charges										
Service increment for teaching and research										
Total income										
Direct Expenditure										
Pay (analysed by grade)										
Non-pay (subjective analysis of direct costs)										
Clinical costs										
Internal recharges for support services										
Medical services										
Radiology										
Pathology										
Non-medical services										
Cleaning										
Porters										
General										
Total expenditure										

Table 8.2 Ward budget

Budget details Whole time Staff numbers	Budget heading	1997/98 Revised budget £	Projected spend to Jan 1998 £	Actual spend to Jan 1998 £	Variance overspend (underspend) £
	Pay				
3	Ward sisters	54,000	45,000	44,000	(1,000)
8	Staff nurses	96,000	80,000	81,200	1,200
12	Assistant nurses	120,000	100,000	96,000	(4,000)
2	Clerical assistants	16,000	13,333	13,000	(333)
	National Insurance				
	Ward sisters	5,400	4,500	4,400	(100)
	Staff nurses	9,600	8,000	8,120	120
	Assistant nurses	12,000	10,000	9,600	(400)
	Clerical assistants	1,600	1,333	1,300	(33)
	Ward Supplies				
	Drugs and dressings	15,000	12,500	13,000	500
	Consumables	7,000	5,833	6,000	167
	Ward sundries	4,800	4,000	3,800	(200)
		341,400	284,499	280,420	(4,079)

If there is a potential shortfall between expenditure and income, then the directorate may look to renegotiate its contracts, or seek efficiency savings to bring the expenditure closer to the level of income available to that directorate. This is where you have to consider the balance between emergency and non-emergency work: the clinical priorities within a department, and the differences between elective and non-elective surgery. In the same way, the introduction of a new drug may trigger off more demand for a particular type of treatment, and if you are funded according to previously lower levels of treatment, you have either to acquire more funds to treat more patients, or restrict the number of patients treated, simply because the funding is not there.

Cost Pressures

One of the terms used in the context of directorates' spending plans is that of 'cost pressures'. This can mean a number of things. One type of cost pressure is the inflationary cost of drugs: for example, some drugs are expensive to produce, and manufacturers may increase their prices in order to recover their costs, particularly if demand for the drug is falling. That is an external cost pressure, imposed from outside the hospital, by a drug manufacturer. Another cost pressure is where changes in clinical practice recommend new drugs being used in areas where there is no base budget for this kind of development. So extra spending is a cost pressure. If you imagine a budget being a fixed amount of money available for a directorate for a period of a year, a more expensive drug or a new drug may take up money in the budget at a faster rate than money was used in the past, and the effect is that in the current conditions you either have to modify your caseload to stay within budget, or keep the same level of activity and overspend. Overspending in one directorate can cause problems in another, so the collective pressure is really to stay within budget, and this means reducing activity accordingly, until more resources can be negotiated or found to restore the planned level of activity.

Devolved Management

The reason for finance being an important consideration is that it is a means of measuring the plans and objectives of directorates, within the environment of business planning and agreed objective setting at the senior decision-making level of the Trust. If information is available at directorate level, then corrective action can be taken to ensure that the whole hospital's spending is in line with its plans.

Financial information is considered both strategically for the hospital as a whole, and managerially at the level of business planning, at directorate level. The use of financial information acts both as a planning mechanism, and as a control mechanism. Putting money values on activity helps to identify how much activity is expected, and as the year passes by and money has been used up, you also have an indication of how much money is left and how much activity can be afforded in the remaining time before a new year and a new budget are in place.

Nothing in the health service stands still: the challenge of the 1990s has been to expand service, to improve patient care and patient outcomes, and to maintain and enhance services through advances in technology and in treatment. The managers and clinicians have been drawn together more by new approaches to organisation and delivery of services, and improved financial awareness has been one of the prerequisites of people achieving high levels of responsibility in the health service. It is hoped that this book will help current students to experiment and discuss their understanding of the linkages between delivery and the need to monitor and control the levels of activity within hospitals, using financial information as one of those indicators.

Appendix

Table of discounting factors for calculating the net present value for capital projects

Present value of £1 received after n years discounted at i%

i n	1	2	3	4	5	6	7	8	9	10
1	.9901	.9804	.9709	.9615	.9524	.9434	.9346	.9259	.9174	.9091
2	.9803	.9612	.9426	.9246	.9070	.8900	.8734	.8573	.8417	.8264
3	.9706	.9423	.9151	.8890	.8638	.8396	.8163	.7938	.7722	.7513
4	.9610	.9238	.8885	.8548	.8227	.7921	.7629	.7350	.7084	.6830
5	.9515	.9057	.8626	.8219	.7835	.7473	.7130	.6806	.6499	.6209
6	.9420	.8880	.8375	.7903	.7462	.7050	.6663	.6302	.5963	.5645

i n	11	12	13	14	15	16	17	18	19	20
1	.9009	.8929	.8850	.8772	.8696	.8621	.8547	.8475	.8403	.8333
2	.8116	.7929	.7831	.7695	.7561	.7432	.7305	.7182	.7062	.6944
3	.7312	.7118	.6931	.6750	.6575	.6407	.6244	.6068	.5934	.5787
4	.6587	.6355	.6133	.5921	.5718	.5523	.5337	.5158	.4987	.4823
5	.5935	.5674	.5428	.5194	.4972	.4731	.4561	.4371	.4190	.4019
6	.5346	.5066	.4803	.4556	.4323	.4104	.3910	.3704	.3521	.3349

Glossary of Terms

These definitions describe accounting and financial terms, and relate both to the private sector and the National Health Service.

Account   A record of one or more transactions of the same type to enable a total to be ascertained, relating to a period, such as a week, a month, a year.

Accountancy   The process of analysing, classifying and recording transactions in terms of time, quantity and money.

Accounting period   The period for which records are kept (also known as the financial year).

Accounting system   The method by which transactions are recorded and which produces summaries for use by internal management. Systems may be stand alone, based on a single department or integrated by the use of common systems across an authority.

Accrual accounting   The basis on which accounts in the private sector are prepared. This recognises a commitment at the point at which it is entered into. Consequently, if by the end of a financial period, the item has not been paid for in full, the outstanding amount is calculated, and called an 'accrual', and is added to the actual spending of that period, so that the full cost of services or goods is recorded. This is sometimes known as the 'matching principle'; where an organisation is not satisfied with a record of receipts and payments, but requires a true picture of actual levels of activity, and the costs incurred in running the organisation, which consist of both 'payments and 'accruals', that is, money which has been handed over, plus bills which are outstanding, but which relate to the financial period even though they are not paid.

Glossary of Terms

Advice note   A note accompanying the delivery of goods which confirms the details of the delivery (sometimes described as the despatch or delivery note).

Age analysis   A term used in credit control. A schedule or list of amounts owing to an organisation, which shows the amount involved and the length of time for which the item has been unpaid.

Amortisation   The writing off of the cost of a certain type of asset, for example the cost of a lease, where the expense involved is caused by the passage of time.

Analyse   The process of classifying and aggregating similar types of transaction under a particular heading which describes the nature of the expenditure, for example to collect together all gas bills under the heading 'heating and lighting'.

Asset   Goods, resources and property of all kinds which the business or organisation intends to keep for the purpose of running the business.

Audit   An independent examination of the accounts and records maintained by an organisation, to establish whether stated policies have been carried out, and to express an opinion on the state of the records.

Auditor   The person who conducts the audit.

Balance (noun)   The difference which exists between two sides of an account, which represents the present state of that account.

Balance (verb)   To prepare a total for both sides of an account, and to calculate the difference, or the resulting figure, which represents the excess of one side over the other.

Balance sheet   A financial statement showing the assets, liabilities and capital at a financial year end, indicating to the owners, shareholders or other interested parties the financial state of the organisation in terms of what it owns and what it owes at that particular time.

Bank reconciliation   The process of listing unpresented cheques and deposits which have not yet shown up on a bank statement, and adjusting for differences between the records kept by the customer, and by the bank, so that both records agree.

Glossary of Terms

Book keeping
The technique of keeping accounts; of recording in a regular, concise and accurate way the transactions of an organisation or a business.

Capital
The initial starting amount of money in a business or enterprise, put in by the owners or their financial supporters in order for the business to acquire the assets or resources with which to run the business. Capital represents the stake in the business attributable to the owners. It is increased by profits, and reduced by withdrawals taken by the owners. In a limited company situation, capital may be 'subscribed' by shareholders, and the value of their stake will fluctuate according to the fortunes of the company. The withdrawals are taken in the form of dividends. In the National Health Service, the capital needed to run the scale of the service is provided from the proceeds of national taxation, and the growth of the service depends on the amounts decided by Parliament in the annual review of expenditure. Capital in the context of health authorities is a cash sum made available by the Department of Health through the Treasury, and represents a direct investment by central government in health facilities. In a Trust situation, capital is inherited from predecessor authorities and the burden of debt associated with those assets becomes the responsibility of the trust to finance.

Capitation-based funding
Each region's population is weighted to reflect demands placed on health services by different age groups. These rates are based on the estimated expenditure per head for different age groups. These age-weighted populations are adjusted by the standardised mortality rate. Certain geographical supplements are built into the allocations, for example special funds for London due to the predominance of teaching hospitals, and the prevalence of certain types of illness.

Cash limits
Spending plans are expressed in cash terms, assuming a predicted level of inflation. If pay and price rises are in excess of the estimates built into the cash-limited figure, then there is no promise that extra money will be provided. The cash limit therefore becomes an effective ceiling to the activities of the organisation.

Close off/ close down	To carry out the final accounting entries relating to a financial period; to transfer details of expenditure and income to an annual statement (the revenue account in the case of the public sector, and the profit and loss account in the case of the private sector).
Contra	A Latin word meaning 'against'. The matching of one item against another: for example, cancelling a debt due from one person, by setting against it an amount which is due to that person. One entry cancels out the other hence 'contra'.
Core services	Those services, such as accident and emergency services, to which patients need local access and where there is no sensible alternative provision available.
Cost and volume contracts	The provider recovers a sum in return for treating a specified number of cases.
Cost per case contracts	The purchaser agrees the price to be paid for the treatment of individual patients.
Credit (noun)	An entry on the right-hand side of a ledger.
Credit (verb)	To 'credit' is to make an entry on the right-hand side.
Credit note	A document sent to a person, firm or organisation, confirming that the account is credited with the amount stated (for example when goods are returned by that person, firm and so on, or when an allowance is made to that person, firm and so on).
Creditor	One to whom money is owed for supplies, goods, services and so on.
Current assets	A description covering a group of different things which are assets in a reasonably realisable state: for example bank balances, cash, stores, stock items, debtors and so on.
Debit (noun)	An entry on the left-hand side of a ledger account.
Debit (verb)	To 'debit' an account is to make an entry on the left-hand side.
Debit note	A document sent to a person, company and so on, stating that their account has been charged with the amount stated. For example, goods ordered by phone, and for which the debit note acts as confir-

	mation that the items have been charged to the person or organisation from whom the order emanated.
Debtor	A person who owes money for goods, or services supplied but not paid for.
Depreciation	The estimated loss in value of an asset due to its use, and charged as a deduction or charge against revenues of a particular period.
Discount	A deduction from the amount due under an invoice; for example a trade discount is an allowance granted to a purchaser who is entitled to some special treatment by the supplier, for example a supplier of lighting fittings may grant a trade discount to those firms which regularly stock their products, and the difference between the catalogue or selling price and the price of the item to the purchaser represents the 'trade discount'.
	A 'settlement discount' is a reduction in the size of the final bill as a 'thank you' for prompt or early settlement of the bill.
Double entry	A method of book keeping in which two entries are made for each transaction in order to record the two aspects which every transaction has and to enable the proof of entries by balancing the ledgers in which each aspect is recorded.
Endowment funds	Derived from donations or from legacies, and must be used in accordance with the express purposes of the fund.
Extra-contractual referrals	These are known as ECRs. They represent non-predictable referrals, either emergency or non-emergency. Purchasers are obliged to pay for emergency treatments, but for non-emergency cases the provider is required to obtain approval from the purchaser before the treatment commences.
Final accounts	The statements prepared to summarise and record the results of a financial period.
Fixed asset	An asset which is in permanent use within a firm, company, business or organisation.
Fixed cost	Fixed costs remain unchanged as output or activity increases. For example, if an ambulance Trust rented a garage for overnight storage of vehicles,

the cost of that expenditure would be regarded as a fixed cost, as whether there were two, five or no ambulances in the garage, the rent would still be the same figure in terms of outgoings of the Trust to the landlord. If, at a later date, new vehicles were ordered, and more garaging was needed, then there would be a second amount of fixed cost added to the original level. If costs rise in this way, they are known as 'stepped costs'.

GP fundholders

Certain approved general practices became responsible for budgets for certain non-emergency health treatment and will act as purchasers of services. The allocation to a practice is made up of three parts:

● practice staff reimbursement

● selected hospital services

● drugs.

Funding is transferable by the practice between heads, and savings can be carried forward from one financial year to another. Savings can be spent on further services, but cannot be used directly to benefit individual fundholding GPs.

Gross

A total without any deductions, for example 'gross pay' is the total amount of pay a person is entitled to, before taking off any deductions.

Grossing up

The calculation of a gross figure from a net figure by adding on the deductions already made in arriving at the net figure.

Impersonal accounts

Accounts not dealing with persons but other things, for example 'real' accounts containing details of property, and 'nominal' accounts dealing with expenses and revenues.

Imprest system

A method in which a pre-determined sum is given to a budget holder for small items of expenditure, and these outgoings are periodically reimbursed so that the imprest holder has the amount of cash restored to the original level.

Intangible asset

An asset which is neither fixed nor current yet which possesses an intrinsic value, for example a brand name.

Glossary of Terms

Inventory	A listing of items owned by an organisation, usually applied to stock, and to which values are applied, so that the organisation can trace its own assets.
Invoice	A document showing the character, quantity, price, terms, address for delivery and other particulars of goods sold or services supplied.
Joint funding/ joint finance	An initiative of the central government which began in the mid-1970s to encourage the working together of health authorities and local authorities, whereby in return for an injection of money from central government, both the local health and local government unit would take an initiative to develop or extend services; most of the initiatives concentrated on mental illness, mental handicap or elderly population over 75 years of age. Funding was for five or seven years with a tapering effect, during which time the responsibility for future financing would pass from the government to a local authority or a voluntary or charitable body.
Journal	A means of recording transactions which is commonly used in the health service for adjustments of money between departments. Journal transfers are internal adjustments which obviate the need to draw a cheque, as the transfer of money is within the same organisation.
Large capital schemes	Are controlled by regional authorities and cover major building work and medical equipment costing over £50,000.
Ledger	A collection of accounts. A general ledger contains a summary of all the principal accounts which form the basis of the annual accounts. A creditors' ledger contains details of transactions with suppliers, and a debtors' ledger contains details of transactions affecting customers.
Ledger account	A record in the ledger showing one of the two aspects of each transaction or group of transactions.
Liabilities	A general heading under which are recorded amounts owing to suppliers (creditors), expenses (accruals) and debts owing by the firm or organisation.

Liquidity	The excess of cash or current assets over current liabilities. ('Current' in this context means repayable within the next 12 months.)
Materiality	A consideration of the significance of an amount in relation to the context in which it is placed. In relation to accounts, an amount is not material if its effect on the accounts would not distort the overall truth and fairness of the view they give.
Minor capital schemes	Are controlled by District Health Authorities, and are in respect of:

- medical equipment
- vehicles
- minor building work and alterations
- fire precautions
- staff accommodation
- other similar schemes.

Net	The amount of any charge or cost after all deductions have been taken out.
Nominal accounts	Accounts for the income (and expenses) of an organisation.
Nominal ledger	An alternative term for the general ledger.
Non-core services	Those services for which health authorities have scope for exercising choice.
Personal account	An account showing transactions with a particular person, firm or company, as distinct from a nominal account.
Petty cash	A system for dealing with small payments, in which a budget holder or similarly authorised person is given a small amount of funds out of which minor payments can be made. Periodically, the fund is replenished up to the original amount, by reimbursing expenditure. This is known as the 'imprest' system of petty cash.
Posting	The transfer of entries from one record to another.
Prepayment	A payment made in the accounting period which relates to goods or services of a future period. For example, an insurance premium usually lasts for a full year. If part of the premium goes beyond the

financial year end, then that part is regarded as a prepayment.

Profit and loss account
A summary account of all the revenue and expenses for a period, and the difference between income and expenditure for that period.

Provider role
To deliver contracted services within quality and quantity specifications to one or a number of purchasers in return for agreed charges.

Provisions (as an expense)
A term which is used as a description for the purchase of food for use within an organisation; for example in a hospital, provisions indicates the cost of meat, flour, fish and groceries, which are then converted into meals.

Provisions (in the context of final accounts)
Amounts written off or retained out of profits to provide for the depreciation, renewal or diminution of assets, or retained to provide for any known liability of which the amount cannot be determined with accuracy.

Purchasing role
Within available resources, services are secured to meet the health needs of the purchaser's resident population.

Reconcile (verb)
To ascertain the precise components of the difference between two related figures produced independently of each other.

Reconciliation
A statement showing the process whereby the balances of two accounts, which have been prepared in respect of the same transactions, have been agreed. For example, a bank reconciliation compares the records kept by the organisation with the records or statement provided by the bank, and agrees the two by allowing for timing differences in the depositing of money and the presentation of cheques.

Revenue
Income received or generated from any source.

Schedule
A detailed list of items totalled to agree with a figure that has been analysed and cross-referenced.

Semi-variable costs
Costs which are partly fixed, and partly vary with usage, for example a telephone bill is fixed in regard to the line rental charge, and variable in relation to the call charges.

Statement of account	An account, periodically rendered, showing the amounts due by one person or firm to another. Generally, a statement contains only the dates and amounts of each invoice sent since the previous settlement.
Stock	The value of items which have been acquired but not used, for example amounts of stationery, drugs, dressings and provisions. These are usually valued at the lower of cost or net realisable value.
Suspense account	An unexplained item or series of items, which are temporarily not included in the accounts until their exact nature has been discovered.
Total (or control) accounts	An account which acts as a summary of all the items debited or credited to a number of individual accounts in a ledger, so that the total account may represent the individual accounts in providing a single figure in summary instead of a whole series of figures. A total or control account is often used in payroll, to check the accuracy of a great number of transactions before the final net pay is released from the organisation. Total accounts support the work which has been done in detail, and are complementary to the detailed work. They are a means of proving the accuracy of detailed work in an independent way.
Transfer	An amount taken from one account and reinstated in another.
Trial balance	A summary listing all the balances in a ledger.
Turnover	The total sales or revenue generated by a business or organisation.
Variable costs	Those costs which increase as the number of patients or type of activity increases. Thus, the cost of plaster in a fracture clinic will increase proportionately to the number of new patients handled by the clinic. Some costs will not alter according to the number of patients, and these should be excluded from the variable costs; for example heating and lighting will be the same and will not vary with throughput of patients.
Writing off	The closing of an account or part of an account by charging debt to the revenue account, or profit and loss account, as irrecoverable. Strict rules governing

Glossary of Terms

the circumstances in which amounts can be written off are usually in place in an authority's financial regulations, to avoid the loss of money through unauthorised cancellation of amounts owing.

Writing up Increasing the value of an asset by making appropriate entries in the books of account.

Further Advanced Reading

Texts

For readers who wish to take the subject further, these texts contain discussion and illustrations of health service finance, and capital and revenue budgeting.

Bailey D (1994) *The NHS Budget Holder's Survival Guide*, The Royal Society of Medicine Press, London.

Coombs HM and Jenkins DE (1996) *Public Sector Financial Management*, 2nd edn, International Thomson Business Press, London.

Doyle D (1994) *Cost Control: A Strategic Guide*, Kogan Page, London.

Drury C (1996) *Management and Cost Accounting*, 4th edn, International Thomson Business Press, London.

Glynn JJ, Perrin J and Murphy MP (1995) *Accounting for Managers*, Chapman & Hall, London.

Jackson PM and Lavender M (1997) *The Public Services Yearbook*, Pitman Publishing, London. (Annual).

Jones B (1996) *Financial Management in the Public Sector*, McGraw-Hill, Maidenhead.

Jones R and Pendlebury M (1996) *Public Sector Accounting*, 4th edn, Pitman Publishing, London.

Mellett H, Marriott N and Harries S (1993) *Financial Management in the NHS: A Manager's Handbook*. Chapman & Hall, London.

Scottish Office, National Health Service in Scotland Management Executive (1996) *NHS Trusts: Guidance for Finance Managers*. HMSO, Edinburgh.

Research Papers

Bourne M and Sutcliffe C (eds) (1996) *Management Accounting in Health-care*, The Chartered Institute of Management Accountants, London.

Lapsley I, Llewellyn S and Burnett G (1998) *Inside Hospital Trusts: Management Styles, Accounting Constraints*, The Institute of Chartered Accountants of Scotland, Edinburgh. (Research report).

Purdey DE (1994) *Cash Budgets and the Psychology of Managing Healthcare in the NHS*, Discussion papers in accounting, finance and banking, No. 39, University of Reading, Department of Economics, Reading.

Sutcliffe CMS (1997) *Developing Decision Support Systems: A Study of Healthcare Management*, The Chartered Institute of Management Accountants, London.

Magazine Articles and Journals

Bailey D (1995) Getting your money's worth out of your accountant, *British Journal of Health Care Management*, **3**(4): 215–17.

Bailey D (1995) Take control of your budget, *Nursing Management*, **1**(8): 16–17.

Bailey D (1995) Wage war on your budget, *Nursing Management*, **1**(9): 22–3.

Bailey D (1996) Budgeting skills, *Nursing Standard*, **10**: 43–6.

Cavouras CA and McKinley J (1997) Variable budgeting for staffing: analysis and evaluation, *Nursing Management (US)*, **28**(5): 34, 36, 39.

Cook A (1995) Management accounting, *British Medical Journal*, **310**: 381–5.

Craske C (1997) Cash control, *Nursing Times*, **93**: 69–71.

Lapsley I (1994) Responsibility accounting revived? Market reforms and budgetary control in healthcare, *Management Accounting Research*, **5**(3/4): 337–52.

Marriott DN and Mellett HJ (1995) The level of skills of National Health Service managers, *Financial Accountability and Management*, **11**(3): 271–82.

Marriott N and Mellett H (1996) Perceived quality of management information and the influence of overspending penalties in the NHS, *Health Services Management Research*, **9**(4): 254–61.

Murphy MP and Perkins DA (1995) Devolved budgetary management systems: means, ends, or myth? *British Journal of Health Care Management*, **1**(6): 283–5.

Further Advanced Reading

Pilkington S (1997) Year to end budget forecasting, income and expenditure, *British Journal of Hospital Medicine*, **57**(10): 527–30.

Sengin KK and Dreisbach AM (1995) Managing with precision: a budgetary decision support model, *Journal of Nursing Administration (US)*, **25**(2): 33–44.

Woodgates P (1995) Multiple division, *Health Service Journal*, **105**: 28–30.

Index

Index

Financial Management

ESSENTIALS OF NURSING MANAGEMENT